Three Little Pigs
and
One Big Pig

Written by Deana Kirk
Illustrated by Suçie Stevenson

Once upon a time, there were
three little pigs and one big pig.

The three little pigs liked to play.

But the big pig just liked to lie in
the mud.

"Let's swim in this puddle!" said the little pigs.

"You go ahead," the big pig said.
"I'll just lie here in the mud."

"Let's push this ball!" said the little pigs.

"You go ahead," the big pig said.
"I'll just lie here in the mud."

"Let's dig, dig, dig!" said the little pigs.

10

"You go ahead," the big pig said.
"I'll just lie here in the mud."

"The wolf!" said the little pigs. "Let's run!"

12

"You go ahead," the big pig said.
"I'll just lie here in the mud."

And he did.